Midnight Journeys

Travels in the Mysterious World of Sleep

Maureen Mecozzi

Contents

Rigby

A Harcourt Achieve Imprint

www.Rigby.com
1-800-531-5015

Chapter 1
Understanding Sleep

You do it every night without even thinking about it. The sun sets, the evening hours pass, a yawn or two sneaks by, and all your muscles whisper: "Get horizontal!" You crawl into bed, as if following orders given by an invisible general. By unspoken command, your eyelids start to droop—how heavy they feel! In a few moments your eyes close, your body relaxes, and your breathing becomes deeper.

And then comes sleep.

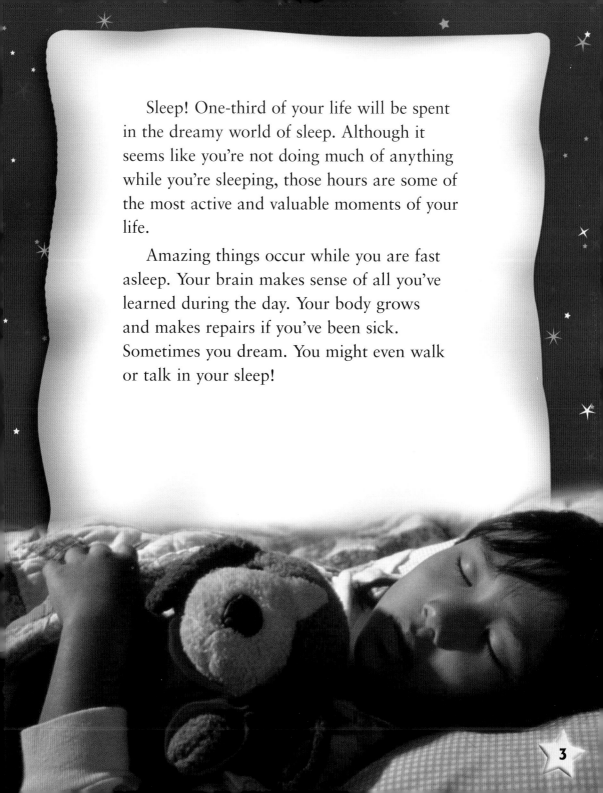

Sleep! One-third of your life will be spent in the dreamy world of sleep. Although it seems like you're not doing much of anything while you're sleeping, those hours are some of the most active and valuable moments of your life.

Amazing things occur while you are fast asleep. Your brain makes sense of all you've learned during the day. Your body grows and makes repairs if you've been sick. Sometimes you dream. You might even walk or talk in your sleep!

What Is Sleep?

Like food or water, we need sleep to live. But what exactly *is* sleep?

We now know that sleep is a state of rest during which you are **conscious** and aware. Your brain is working while you sleep. Your body is aware of what's going on around you. Your vision, hearing, and sense of touch all continue to function. If you gently touch a sleeper's face, he or she will rub near the place it was touched without ever waking up.

For thousands of years, however, people thought nothing much happened during sleep. It was as if the body hung out a sign: "Sleeping—Closed for Business." It wasn't until people began losing sleep that we started asking serious questions about what sleep is.

SLEEPING— CLOSED FOR BUSINESS

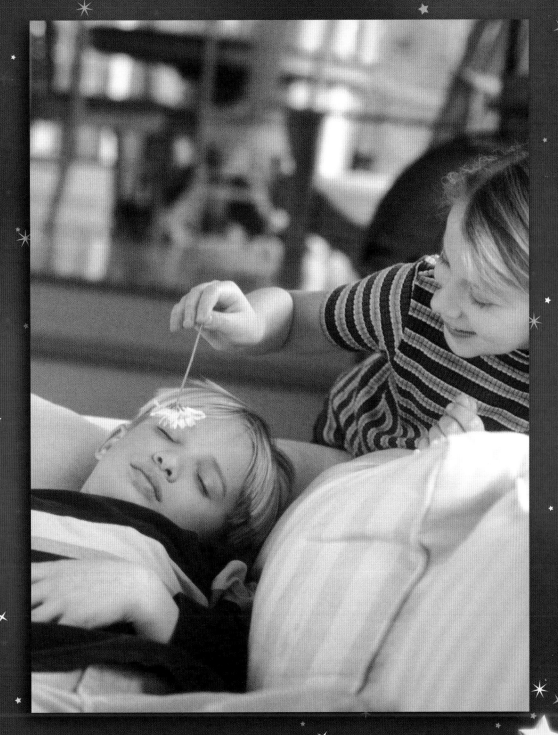

Blame It on the Lightbulb!

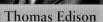
Thomas Edison

After Thomas Edison invented the electric lightbulb, the difference between night and day was nearly erased. The bright electric light, so different from the glow of candlelight or oil lamps, encouraged people to stay awake longer and sleep less. In the morning, they felt tired and cranky, and were more likely to make mistakes on the job.

Scientists and doctors began to study sleep carefully. They discovered that sleep lets the body work on all kinds of important actions needed for human health. Sleep rests the muscles and allows the body to store energy for the waking hours. Sleep helps the body fight illness and heal itself. Without proper sleep, the body won't grow as it should, and the mind will become confused.

They also found that the amount of sleep each person needs varies, depending on age, habits, and the pressure of school and work.

Before electric light, most people slept about 9 hours a night. Today we sleep only about $7\frac{1}{2}$ hours a night. Maybe Mr. Edison's invention wasn't as good a thing as we've believed!

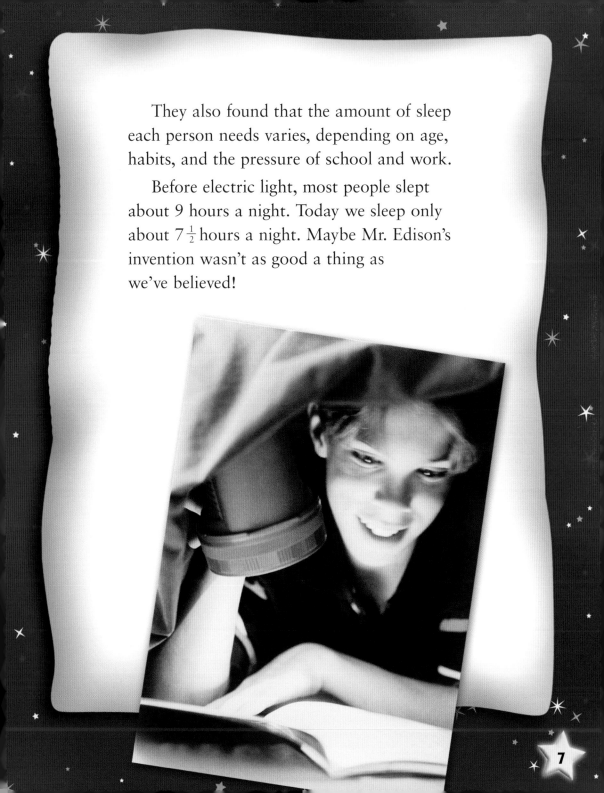

Chapter 2

How Sleep Happens

Have you ever "slept like a rock"? The minute your head hits the pillow, you're out. You sleep so deeply, you don't remember anything—no dreams, not when your parents came in to kiss you goodnight, or how the blankets ended up on the floor!

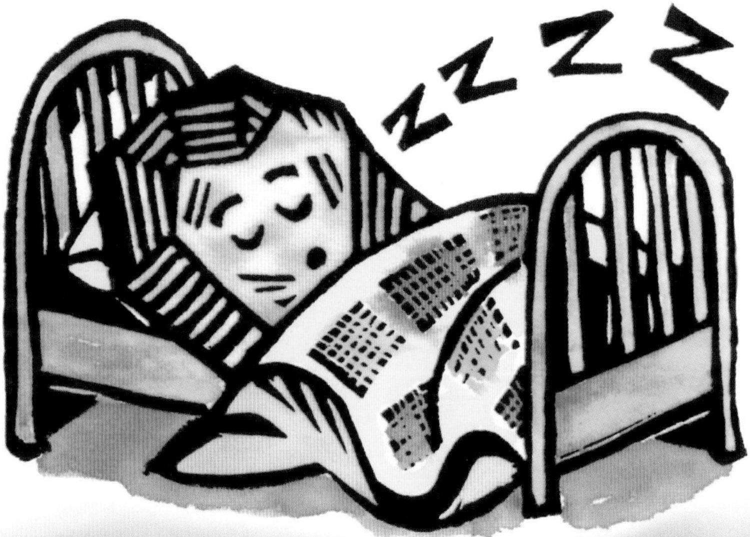
ZZZZZ

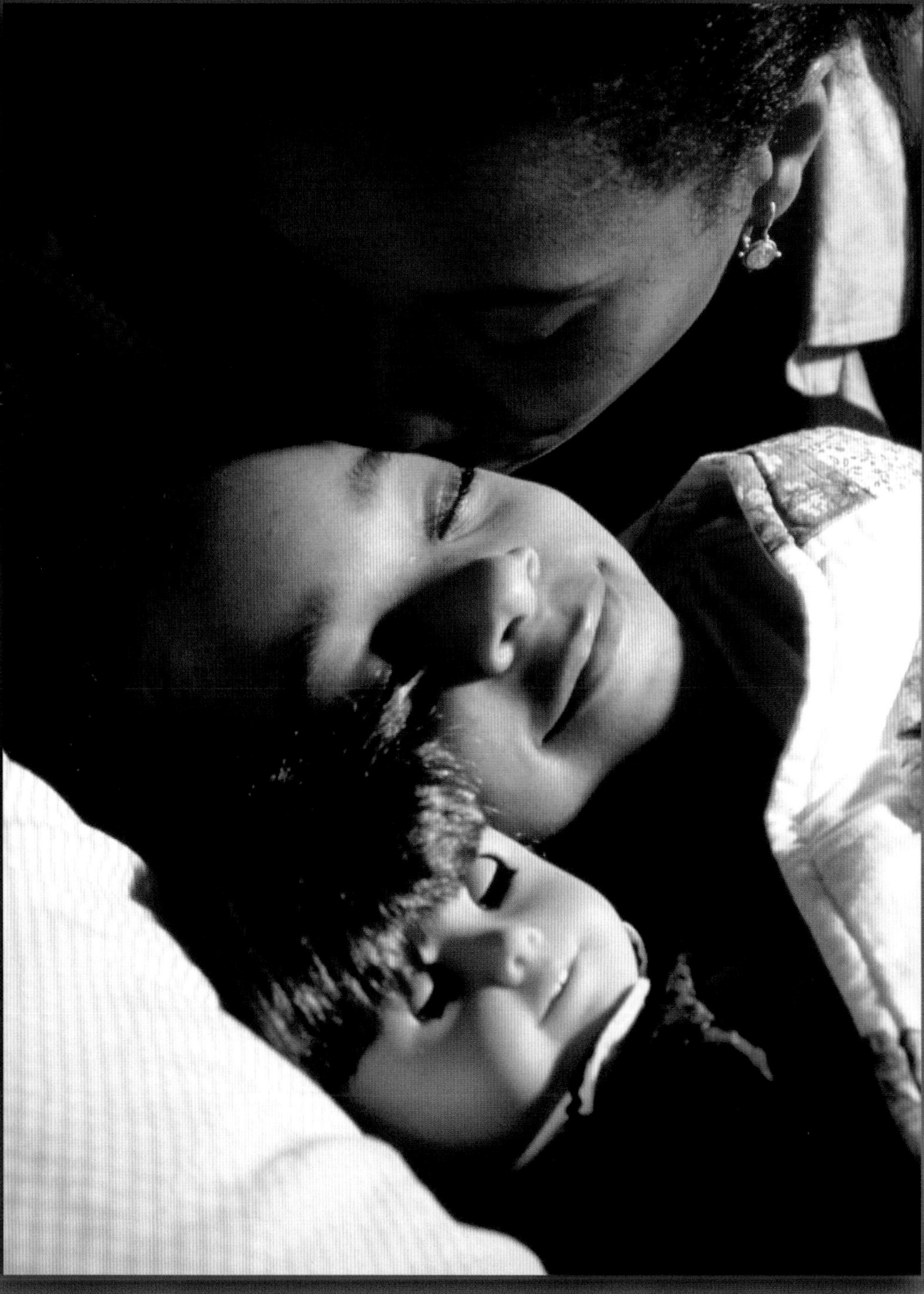

Sleep Comes in Stages and Cycles

It may feel like it sometimes, but sleep isn't one long, uninterrupted event. Instead, sleep comes in stages and cycles.

Stage 1

Your eyes close, your muscles relax, your heartbeat slows down, and your breathing becomes even and steady. You're aware of faint sounds around you. Usually, you're in this stage for 5 to 10 minutes.

Stage 2

For the next 15 to 30 minutes, you're asleep, but just barely. If someone gave you a nudge, or if your dog put its cold nose on your arm, you would quickly wake up.

Stage 3

Next, you spend a few minutes in a fairly deep sleep.

Stage 4

Now comes the deepest sleep stage, lasting from 30 to 40 minutes. Your body is still—there's no tossing and turning—and your breathing is deep and regular. It's difficult to wake someone up during this stage.

Something interesting happens at the end of Stage 4. You change position. You may turn from side to side, or roll over from your back onto your stomach. You go into a lighter sleep. And then you begin REM (Rapid Eye Movement) sleep.

During REM sleep, your eyes dart back and forth beneath your closed eyelids. Your brain is working, just as it is when you are awake. This is the time when you dream! REM sleep lasts from 20 to 30 minutes.

All the stages together are known as "the sleep cycle." One sleep cycle lasts about 90 to 100 minutes, and it is repeated several times a night.

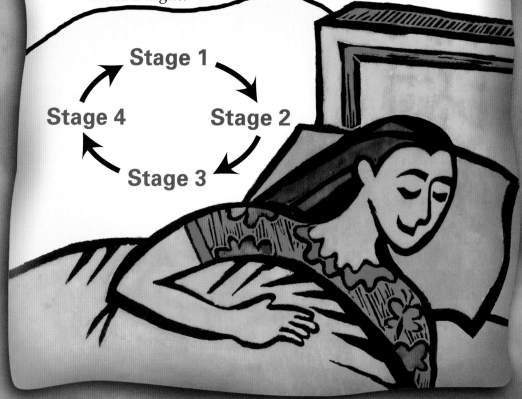

Stage 1

Stage 2

Stage 3

Stage 4

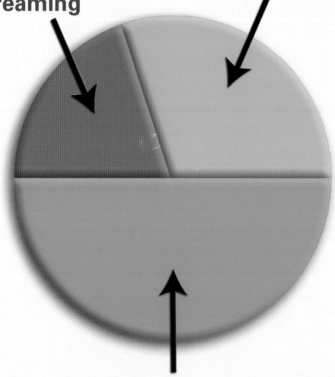

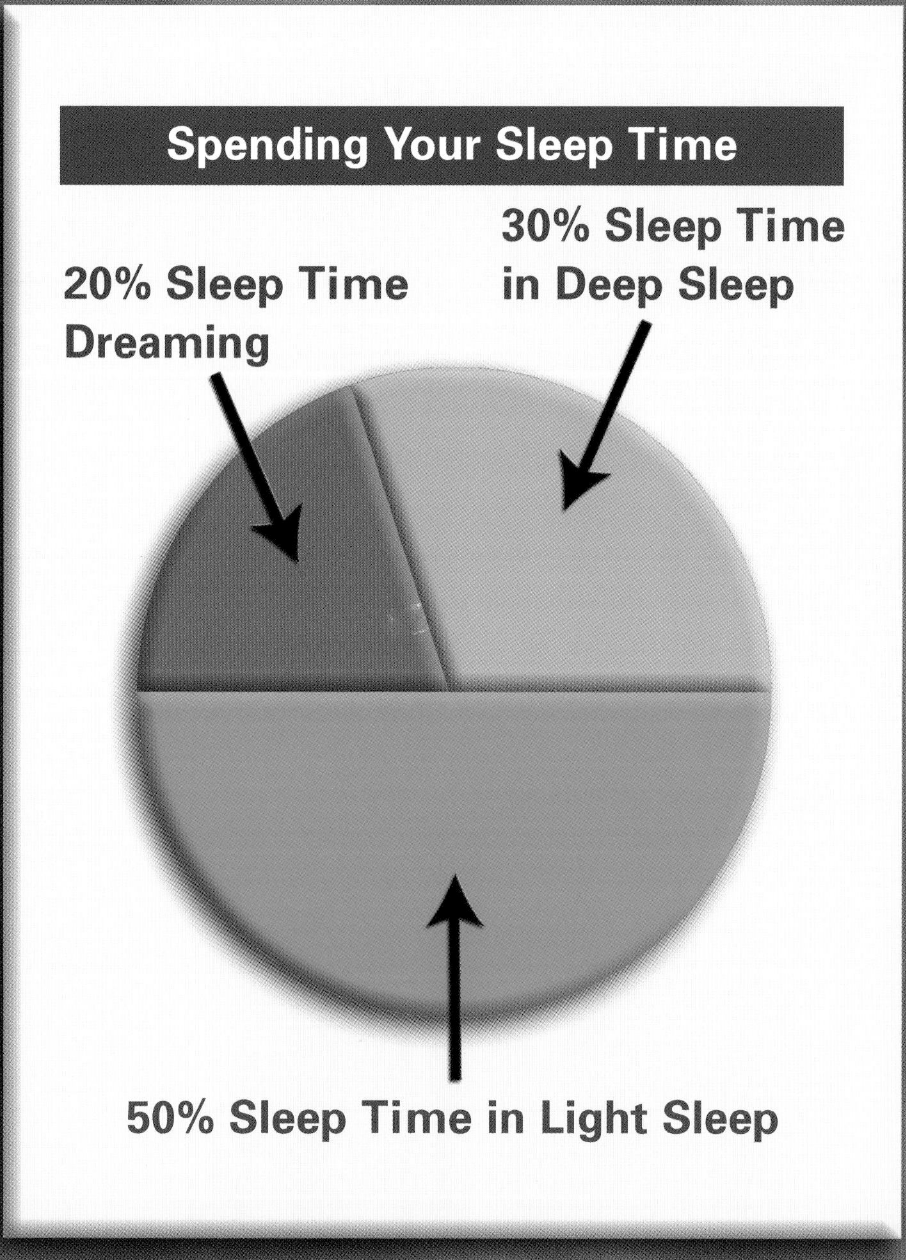

Spending Your Sleep Time

30% Sleep Time in Deep Sleep

20% Sleep Time Dreaming

50% Sleep Time in Light Sleep

Some Need More, Some Need Less

The amount of sleep you need to stay healthy changes as you grow older.

If you have a baby brother or sister, you know they do almost nothing but sleep! Babies snooze on and off between 16 and 20 hours a day. For nearly half that time, a baby dreams. That's why you can see a lot of movement under a sleeping baby's closed eyelids. With so many new experiences to understand, a baby's brain must work hard, even during sleep.

Toddlers sleep about 10 to 12 hours a day, usually sleeping through the night and having a nap in the afternoon.

Older children and teenagers need about 9 to 11 hours of sleep a night. Today, however, few kids get that much sleep. After-school activities, homework, sports, TV, and the Internet push back bedtimes later and later. The morning schedule hasn't changed, though. You've still got to get up early for school!

The average 12-year-old sleeps only $8\frac{1}{2}$ hours a night. The average teen sleeps even less. Kids who "cheat" on sleep have a difficult time waking up in the morning. They're often sluggish and tired in class.

Adults today need 8 to 9 hours of sleep, but most sleep only about $7\frac{1}{2}$ hours a night; that's why your parents might like to "sleep in" on weekends! Older people sleep more lightly and for fewer hours a night than middle-aged adults. Because they are such light nighttime sleepers, older people often take several short daytime naps.

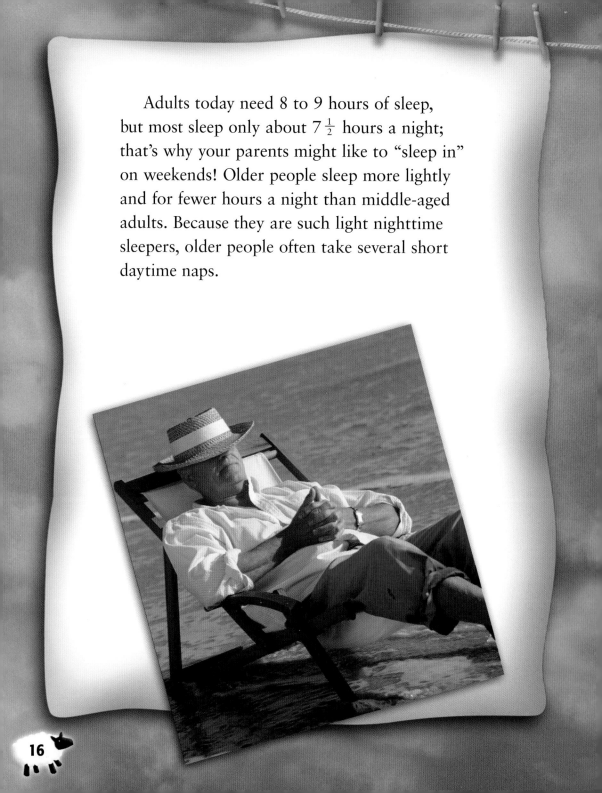

Sleep? Nah!

Plenty of people would gladly trade in their pajamas and skip sleep altogether! They believe the time spent sleeping could be put to better use. They forget how important sleep is to our overall health and well-being.

Still, some people do manage to get along on a lot less sleep than normal. Thomas Edison said he never needed more than 4 or 5 hours of sleep per night. (No wonder he invented the light bulb . . . he didn't like spending all that time in the dark!)

Chapter 3
Rest Easy!

What is a dream? A sleep scientist will tell you that a dream is the brain's review of your life. The things that are important to you—family, friends, sports, schoolwork, maybe even your goldfish—turn up again and again in your dreams. During a dream, the brain is awake, storing and sorting all of the experiences of the day and the previous week or so. The brain can be so lively during a dream that you may actually feel like you're running or swimming or shouting, or that you're hot, cold, or hungry.

Nightmares are scary dreams, but don't be afraid. Remember, they're only dreams—they're not real.

Do you remember any of your dreams? They often don't make sense, but sometimes they do make a good story!

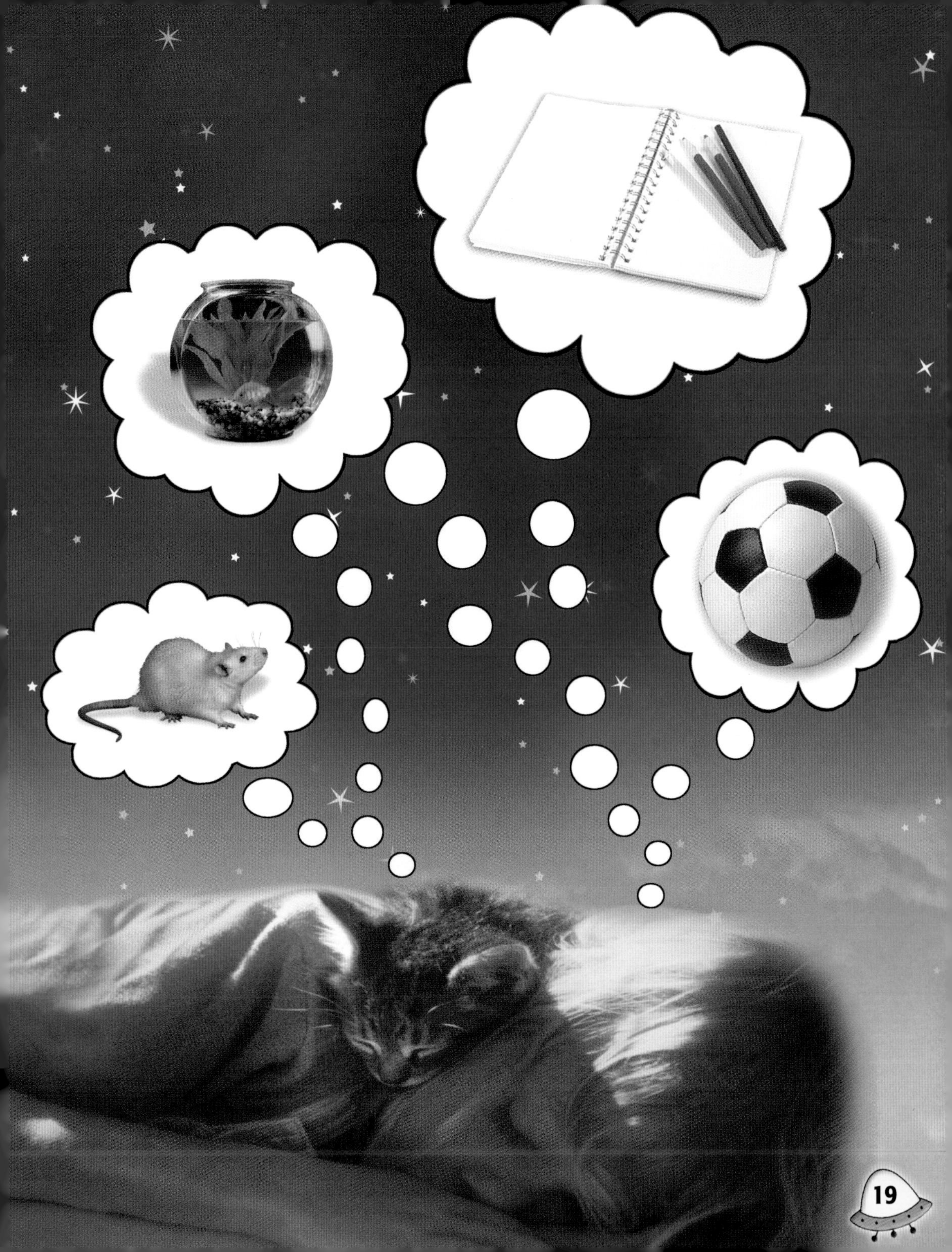

Strange Sleep Habits

Are you someone who likes to take a late-night stroll . . . in your pajamas? *Sleepwalking* is a strange experience that is more common for children than adults. It occurs during very deep sleep. The brain decides that it's time for a walk, and the body responds. Sleepwalkers get up out of bed and go walking through the house. They may look like they are awake, but they aren't. They have blank, staring faces, don't respond when others try to communicate, and are difficult to wake up. Once they do wake up, they might not remember anything about their midnight wanderings. Since sleepwalking happens during deep sleep, don't bother trying to wake up a sleepwalker. Just point him or her back in the direction of the bed!

Some people talk in their sleep. *Sleep talking*, like sleepwalking, happens when you're sleeping deeply, or when you're in the middle of an intense dream. You can chatter all night long, but the next morning, you might not remember a word of what you said.

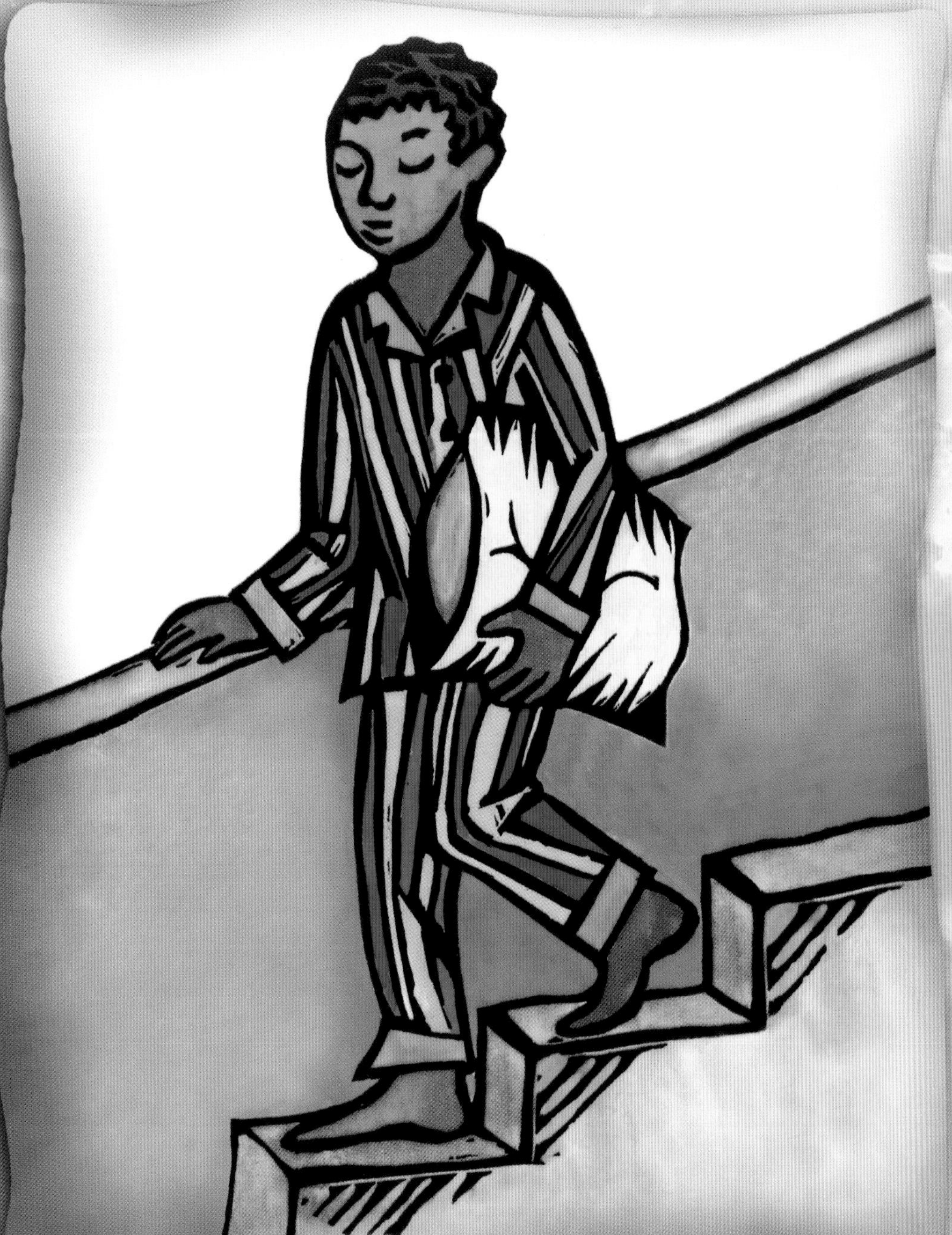

Sleep Problems

Everybody snores at one time or another. It could be a soft, gentle rumbling—or an earthshaking, elephant-thundering clatter! Snoring occurs when something blocks the free flow of air between the nose and the windpipe. You may snore a little if you have a stuffed-up nose from a cold.

Serious snorers may have a condition known as *sleep apnea*. The airflow is blocked, and the person actually stops breathing for short periods of 10 seconds or so. This uneven breathing interrupts the snorer's sleep patterns and makes it hard to get a good night's rest.

People who suffer from **insomnia** also can't get the rest they need. Insomniacs stay awake night after night, and not by choice. Illness, stress, and other problems keep them from getting the sleep they need.

You may have had nights when you just couldn't sleep, perhaps because you were excited about a trip or holiday, or worried about a test the next day. If you can't sleep, don't stay in bed. Get up, go to a different room, and read, draw, or do something else to relax your mind. Usually, in about 15 or 20 minutes, you'll feel tired and ready for bed.

Narcolepsy is just the opposite of insomnia. People with this rare sleep problem fall asleep anywhere, anytime—while munching on a hot dog, talking on the phone, even while driving a car. Fortunately, doctors can help patients with narcolepsy and other sleep problems by prescribing medicine or recommending changes in diet and exercise.

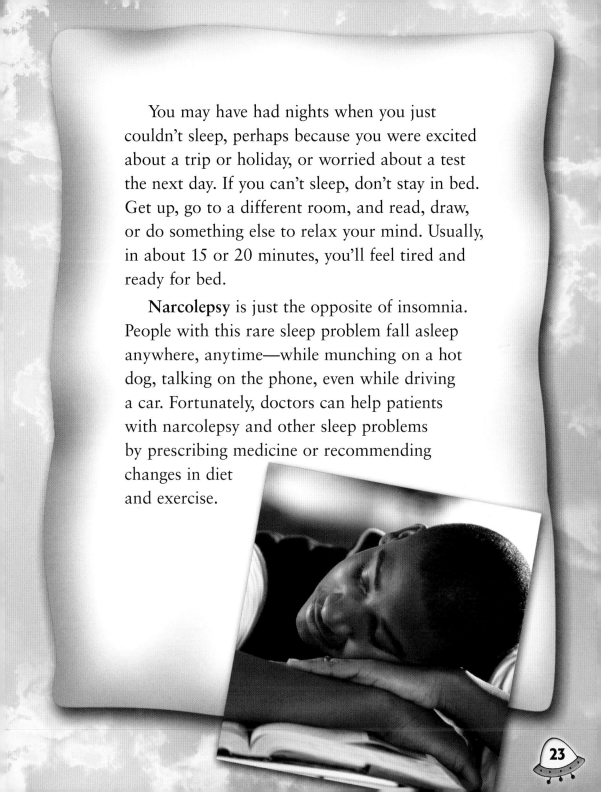

Chapter 4

Elephants and EEGs

Like humans, animals of all kinds need sleep. Grazing animals, like horses, deer, and sheep, sleep about 3 or 4 hours out of every 24. They can snooze standing up, ready to run if they need to get away.

It seems like whales, dolphins, and other sea animals never sleep, because they never stop swimming. But they do log about 7 hours of sleep per day by taking a lot of very short naps that are less than 1 minute in length.

Some birds, like swifts and albatrosses, can sleep while flying, by taking brief naps. Other birds rest when the sun goes down.

Maybe you've seen your pet dog or cat dream: Their paws make a running motion, their faces and whiskers twitch, their eyes move beneath their eyelids, and they may even make sounds. Smaller animals dream more often than larger animals: A mouse dreams every 9 minutes, while an elephant dreams only once every 2 hours.

If a fish has its fins flattened against its body or held out still and unmoving, and if its gills are moving slowly and regularly, it's probably asleep. But you can't tell by looking at its eyes. Fish don't have eyelids, so their eyes don't close when they sleep!

The animal world's champion sleeper is the bat. It spends nearly 20 hours out of every 24 sleeping. Moths, bees, even sea slugs sleep.

Animals and Sleep

Species	Hours of sleep per day
Horse	3
Giraffe	3
Deer	3
Elephant	4
Goat	4
Sheep	4
Cow	4
Dolphin	7
Rabbit	8
Pig	8
Guinea pig	8
Mole	9
Dog	9
Chimpanzee	10
Monkey	10
Baboon	10
Beaver	11
Fox	11
Jaguar	11
Gorilla	12
Wolf	13
Raccoon	13
Rat	13
Mouse	13
Hamster	14
Cat	15
Squirrel	15
Opossum	19
Bat	20

They Sleep Standing Up

How do birds stay on their perches while they sleep? The **tendons** in their legs reach down over the knee, continue down the leg, around the ankle, and then under the toes. At rest, the bird's weight causes it to bend its knees, which pulls the tendons tight and closes the claws tightly around the perch.

Wired for Sleep

How did we learn so much about sleep? We watched people and animals sleep, of course. (Talk about a boring job . . . it's enough to put you to sleep!) The first sleep researchers had people sleep in special beds attached to a device similar to one used to measure earthquakes. The device measured the movements of the bed, which helped researchers understand when people were passing from one sleep stage to the next.

Today researchers explore sleep with a test called an EEG (electroencephalogram). Special wires taped to a sleeper's head measure electrical activity given off by brain waves. Each stage of sleep has a different pattern of brain waves. A sleeper might look weird with all those wires attached, but an EEG doesn't hurt at all, and most importantly, it doesn't interfere with sleep!

Are You a Lark or an Owl?

Larks are birds that are known for their beautiful song, which they often sing early in the morning. Owls sleep during the day and do their hunting in the evening and night. These bird names are used to label people who do their best work early or late in the day. "Larks" are "early birds," people who wake up easily and are at their best in the morning hours. "Owls" work best later in the day and are more active at night. Which are you?

Take a Test!

Circle one:

1. I am most alert during the:

        morning   **evening**

2. I have the most energy during the:

        morning   **evening**

3. I remember things better if I read or hear them in the:

        morning   **evening**

4. I like to play most during the:

        morning   **evening**

5. I feel best if I wake up:

        before 8 AM   **after 8 AM**

If you have three or more answers circled in the morning group, you're a lark. If you have three or more circled in the evening group, you're an owl. Either way, just remember to give your body the sleep it needs!

Glossary

conscious—being aware of one's own thoughts and surroundings

insomnia—can't sleep night after night

narcolepsy—falls asleep at any time, anywhere

tendons—tissue that connects muscles to bones

Index